Julia Joan –

Be kind always!

Erika Lee Krebs

Dedicated to:

Barney, my very first dog, for teaching me
that dogs are truly family.
Bubba, a rescue, who didn't get the chance he deserved.
Thelma and Louise, my rescue dogs, who were my first babies.
All of these dogs are no longer in my life,
but forever in my heart.

ISBN-13: 978-0692489109
ISBN-10: 069248910X
Library of Congress Control Number: 2015911603

Illustrations are charcoal pencil and chalk, reproduced in full color.

"The Adventures of Zozzy and Baz...and Sissy too." Series #1, 2015

Zozzy and Baz Rescue a Dog

from the series
"The Adventures of Zozzy and Baz...and Sissy too."

written and illustrated by
Erika Lee Krebs

Zozzy and Baz love animals. Sissy does too. They have a home with lots of space outside and would love to have a pet to play with in their yard.

Zozzy and Baz like to play with their friends, Niles and Boden, and their pet dog, Cinnamon.

Cinnamon loves to follow the boys everywhere, even when they ride their bikes!

One day, Zozzy and Baz tell their Mommy that they want their own pet dog. Mommy says "That it is a big responsibility."

"Dogs are fun, but they also have needs."

For example, dogs need to be brushed. Zozzy shows his mommy how he gently brushes Sissy's hair. Do you know how to brush your hair?

Dogs also need to be fed food and water. Baz shows Mommy how to set the table. Do dogs need plates? Silverware? Bowls?

Dogs will need a bath. Baz shows Mommy he knows how to get clean! Do you like to take a bath?

Dogs also need to visit the veterinarian for checkups. Veterinarians are doctors for animals. Zozzy and Baz think doctors are neat!

Dogs especially need lots of playtime for exercise. Zozzy and Baz like to play soccer for their playtime.

What do you like to do for playtime?

Mommy and Daddy tell Zozzy, Baz, and Sissy they are superheroes because they are going to rescue a dog.

They are so excited, they do their happy dance! Do you have a happy dance? Let's see!

When they all get in the car, Zozzy is confused. He asks Daddy, "Why are we superheroes?"

Daddy says, "You are superheroes because you are rescuing a dog who needs you at the animal shelter. An animal shelter is where dogs go that don't have a home. They are waiting there to find their forever home and forever family." Zozzy and Baz are so excited to be a superhero and rescue a dog of their own!

When they arrive at the shelter, the first dog they meet is as big as a horse and has leaky lips! This dog is really nice, but he scares Sissy. His drool falls on her and she thinks he will sit on her. Do you think he will sit on her?

The shelter brings out another dog. She is just a puppy and likes to jump. Mommy says she wants one that already knows where to tinkle!

Dogs come in all different size, shapes, and colors!
What kind of doggy do you like?

Do you like big or small? Long hair or short hair?
Silly playful doggy? Gentle snuggly doggy?

The shelter brings out another dog. Zozzy, Baz, and Sissy love him! They finally rescue their new family member and name him Barney. He is perfect.

Daddy buys a shiny red collar that has Barney's name on it and Daddy's phone number. Do you know why Barney has a tag? It's so that if Barney gets lost, someone can call Daddy to return Barney. It's very important that all dogs wear a collar so they can get back to their own family.

When they bring Barney home, Daddy reminds them about the needs of a dog.

So, Zozzy feeds Barney. Barney sure loves to eat!

Barney visits the vet clinic for a checkup. Zozzy and Baz would like to be a veterinarian when they grow up so they can help animals. Can you say veterinarian?

Baz gives Barney a bath. Baz loves spraying the hose and Barney loves playing in the water!

Sissy likes to brush Barney and put bows on his head. Barney doesn't mind since he loves his new family.

Zozzy and Baz like to call their frisbee a flying plate. Barney is really good at fetching the flying plate for playtime exercise. Dogs sure are fun!

Zozzy and Baz are true superheroes because they rescued Barney and gave him a forever home. He is the perfect new family member.

The End

Please visit

www.erikaleekrebs.com

for more information

INGREDIENTS

1 banana, mashed
1/2 cup peanut or almond butter
1 cup rolled oats or quinoa
1/2 cup applesauce
1 1/4 cup whole wheat flour
1 tsp. cinnamon

INSTRUCTIONS

Preheat oven to 350°. In large bowl, mix ingredients together thoroughly.

Knead and roll out dough. Cut into fun shapes. Bake on greased baking sheet for 10-15 minutes or until edges brown. Cool and refrigerate.

Yummy for dogs and kiddos!

71647430R00022

Made in the
USA
Middletown, DE